Bond

English
Assessment Papers

9–10 years
Book 2

Sarah Lindsay

Nelson Thornes

Published in 2007 by:
Nelson Thornes Ltd
Delta Place
27 Bath Road
CHELTENHAM
GL53 7TH
United Kingdom

12 / 10 9 8 7 6 5 4 3 2

A catalogue record for this book is available from the British Library

ISBN 978 1 4085 1590 7

Illustrations by Lisa Smith (c/o Sylvie Poggio Artists Agency)
Page make-up by Greengate Publishing Services, Tonbridge, Kent

Printed and bound in Egypt by Sahara Printing Company

Acknowledgements
The authors and publishers wish to thank the following for permission to use copyright material:

You Can't Be That from THAWING FROZEN FROGS By Brian Patten (Viking 1990). Text copyright © Brian Patten, 1990; A Pack of Liars by Anne Fine (Hamish Hamilton, 1988). Copyright © Anne Fine, 1988; extract from How to run a marathon, Reprinted by permission of HarperCollins Publishers Ltd. © (Cathy Shipton and Liz McColgan)(1997); extract from Questions and Answers: Oceans and Rivers by Barbara Taylor © Kingfisher Publications Plc. Reproduced by permission of the publisher, all rights reserved; extract from War Horse by Michael Morpurgo Text copyright © 1982 Michael Morpurgo. Published by Egmont UK ltd London and used with permission; extract from Plan UK leaflet; reproduced by permission of Plan UK, Registered UK charity No. 276035 (www.plan-uk.org); THE VOYAGE OF THE DAWN TREADER by C.S. Lewis copyright © C.S. Lewis Pte.Ltd. 1952. Extract reprinted by permission; extract from Wordly Wise by Barrie Wade, Ann Wade and Maggie Moore, Storychest 1986; extract from Guardian Newspapers Limited, After 37 years, polar explorer is brought in from the cold by Esther Adley, Copyright Guardian News and Media Limited 2007.

Every effort has been made to trace the copyright holders, but if any have been inadvertently overlooked the publishers will be pleased to make the necessary arrangement at the first opportunity.

What is Bond?

This book is part of the Bond Assessment Papers series for English, which provides **thorough and continuous practice of key English skills** from ages five to thirteen. Bond's English resources are ideal preparation for Key Stage 1 and Key Stage 2 SATs, the 11+ and other selective school entrance exams.

What does this book cover and how can it be used to prepare for exams?

English 9–10 years Book 1 and *Book 2* can be used both for general practice and as part of the run up to 11+ exams, Key Stage 2 SATs and other selective exams. The papers practise comprehension, spelling, grammar and vocabulary work. The coverage is also matched to the National Curriculum and the National Literacy Strategy. It is outside the scope of this book to practise extended and creative writing skills. *Bond The secrets of Writing* provides full coverage of writing skills.

What does the book contain?

- **12 papers** – each one contains 100 questions.

- **Tutorial links throughout** – – this icon appears in the margin next to the questions. It indicates links to the relevant section in *How to do ... 11+ English*, our invaluable subject guide that offers explanations and practice for all core question types.

- **Scoring devices** – there are score boxes in the margins and a Progress Chart on page 68. The chart is a visual and motivating way for children to see how they are doing. It also turns the score into a percentage that can help decide what to do next.

- **Next Steps Planner** – advice on what to do after finishing the papers can be found on the inside back cover.

- **Answers** – located in an easily-removed central pull-out section.

How can you use this book?

One of the great strengths of Bond Assessment Papers is their flexibility. They can be used at home, in school and by tutors to:

- set **timed formal practice** tests – allow about 45 minutes per paper. Reduce the suggested time limit by five minutes to practise working at speed.

- provide **bite-sized chunks** for regular practice
- **highlight strengths and weaknesses** in the core skills
- identify **individual needs**
- set **homework**
- follow a **complete 11+ preparation strategy** alongside *The Parents' Guide to the 11+* (see below).

It is best to start at the beginning and work though the papers in order. If you are using the book as part of a careful run-in to the 11+, we suggest that you also have four other essential Bond resources close at hand:

How to do ... 11+ English: the subject guide that explains all the question types practised in this book. Use the cross-reference icons to find the relevant sections.

The secrets of Comprehension: the practical handbook that clearly shows children how to read and understand the text, understand the questions and assess their own answers.

The secrets of Writing: the essential resource that explains the key components of successful writing.

The Parents' Guide to the 11+: the step-by-step guide to the whole 11+ experience. It clearly explains the 11+ process, provides guidance on how to assess children, helps you to set complete action plans for practice and explains how you can use *English 9–10 years Book 1* and *Book 2* as part of a strategic run-in to the exam.

See the inside front cover for more details of these books.

What does a score mean and how can it be improved?

It is unfortunately impossible to predict how a child will perform when it comes to the 11+ (or similar) exam if they achieve a certain score on any practice book or paper. Success on the day depends on a host of factors, including the scores of the other children sitting the test. However, we can give some guidance on what a score indicates and how to improve it.

If children colour in the Progress Chart on page 68, this will give an idea of present performance in percentage terms. The Next Steps Planner inside the back cover will help you to decide what to do next to help a child progress. It is always valuable to go over wrong answers with children. If they are having trouble with any particular question type, follow the tutorial links to *How to do ... 11+ English* for step-by-step explanations and further practice.

Don't forget the website...!

Visit www.bond11plus.co.uk for lots of advice, information and suggestions on everything to do with Bond, the 11+ and helping children to do their best.

Key words

Some special words are used in this book. You will find them in **bold** each time they appear in the Papers. These words are explained here.

abbreviation	a word or words which are shortened
abstract noun	a word referring to a concept or idea *love*
acronym	a word or letter string made up from the initial letters of other words
adjectival phrase	a group of words describing a noun
adjective	a word that describes somebody or something
adverb	a word that gives extra meaning to a verb
alphabetical order	words arranged in the order found in the alphabet
antonym	a word with a meaning opposite to another word *hot – cold*
clause	a section of a sentence with a verb
collective noun	a word referring to a group *swarm*
compound word	a word made up of two other words *football*
conjunction	a word used to link sentences, phrases or words *and, but*
connective	a word or words that join clauses or sentences
contraction	two words shortened into one with an apostrophe placed where the letter/s have been dropped *do not = don't*
definition	a meaning of a word
dialect	regional variation of vocabulary in the spoken language
diminutive	a word implying smallness *booklet*
future tense	form of a verb showing something that will or may happen
homophone	a word that has the same sound as another but a different meaning or spelling *right/write*
metaphor	an expression in which something is described in terms usually associated with another *the sky is a <u>sapphire</u> sea*
noun	a word for somebody or something
onomatopoeic	a word that echoes a sound associated with its meaning *hiss*
past tense	form of a verb showing something that has already happened
personal pronoun	a pronoun used when writing about ourselves *I, you*
phrase	a group of words that act as a unit
plural	more than one *cats*
possessive pronoun	a pronoun showing to whom something belongs *mine, ours, his, hers, yours, theirs*
prefix	a group of letters added to the beginning of a word *un, dis*
preposition	a word that relates other words to each other – *he sat <u>behind</u> me, the book <u>on</u> the table*
present tense	form of a verb showing something happening now
pronoun	a word used to replace a noun
proper noun	the names of people, places etc. *Ben*
reported speech	what has been said, without using the exact words or speech marks
root word	a word to which prefixes or suffixes can be added to make another word *<u>quick</u>ly*
singular	one *cat*
suffix	a group of letters added to the end of a word *ly, ful*
synonym	a word with the same or very similar meaning to another word *quick – fast*
verb	a 'doing' or 'being' word

You Can't Be That

I told them:
When I grow up
I'm not going to be a scientist
Or someone who reads the news on TV.
No, a million birds will fly through me.   *5*
I'M GOING TO BE A TREE!

They said,
You can't be that. No, you can't be that.

I told them:
When I grow up   *10*
I'm not going to be an airline pilot,
A dancer, a lawyer or an MC.
No, huge whales will swim in me.
I'M GOING TO BE AN OCEAN!

They said,   *15*
You can't be that. No, you can't be that.

I told them:
I'm not going to be a DJ,
A computer programmer, a musician or beautician.
No, streams will flow through me,   *20*
I'll be the home of eagles;
I'll be full of nooks, crannies, valleys and fountains.
I'M GOING TO BE A RANGE OF MOUNTAINS!

They said,
You can't be that. No, you can't be that.   *25*

I asked them:
Just what do you think I am?
Just a child, they said,
*And children always become
At least one of the things*   *30*
We want them to be.

They do not understand me.
I'll be a stable if I want, smelling of fresh hay,
I'll be a lost glade in which unicorns still play.
They do not realise I can fulfil any ambition.   *35*
They do not realise among them
Walks a magician.

Brian Patten

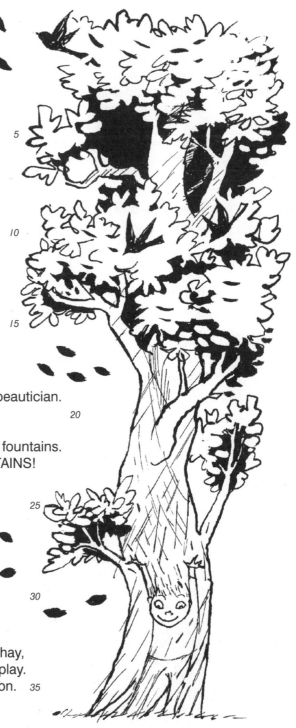

Underline the correct answers.

1 The child wanted to be the home of eagles. What was he going to be?

(a tree, an ocean, a range of mountains)

2 What does the child ultimately want to be?

(a lawyer, a beautician, a magician)

Answer these questions.

3 Find a word in the poem that rhymes with 'tree'. _____

4 Who do you think 'they' (line 7) could be?

_____ adults. _____

5 How does the text indicate when adults are talking?

_____

6–8 Read lines 26–31 again. What impression is given of these adults? How do you think the child might feel?

_____

_____

_____

_____

9–10 Describe the child's character using evidence from the poem.

_____

_____

_____

_____

Write the **plural** form of each of these **nouns**.

11 lantern _____   12 atlas _____

13 disease _____   14 chocolate _____

15 calf _____   16 athlete _____

17 fox _____   18 roof _____

Add a **verb** to complete these sentences. Each verb may be used only once.

D 6

read   searched   ran   went   grew   felt

19 Marcus _____ for the bus.

20 Meena _____ the Internet for information on the Moon.

21 The teacher _____ the chapter to the class.

22 The flowers _____ quickly in the greenhouse.

23 Mr Robson _____ closer to the strange shape.

24 The fire-fighters _____ the force of the explosion.

6

Add the missing punctuation at the end of each sentence.

D 5

25 You should always wear a helmet when riding your bike __

26 The snake slipped silently through the fallen leaves __

27 Quick, we've got to go __

28 Have you done your homework tonight __

29 Hurry, before it starts to rain __

30 What is hiding in the mess under your bed __

31 Queen Victoria served her country for many years __

7

Match to each of these words a word with the same letter string but a different sound.

E 2

plough   argue   nought   glove   wallet   headache   dough   bruise

32 mallet   _____   33 catalogue   _____

34 moustache   _____   35 bough   _____

36 though   _____   37 move   _____

38 disguise   _____   39 drought   _____

8

Underline one word in each group which is not a **synonym** for the rest.

D 9

40 fast   quick   rapid   slow   speedy

41 display   hide   exhibit   demonstrate   reveal

42 guzzle   slurp   quaff   sip   gulp

43 gregarious   lonesome   isolated   remote   solitary

44	angry	sulky	cranky	furious	content
45	misleading	false	accurate	fake	untrue
46	endanger	safeguard	defend	protect	look after

7

D 6

Underline the **pronouns** in the following passage.

47–54 We regretted leaving our jumpers behind. It had become cold and we could have done with <u>them</u> for protection from the biting wind. Still we battled on against the elements. It was so important we made it before darkness fell.

8

D 8

Write the masculine of each of the following words.

55 mistress _____   **56** hen _____

57 sow _____   **58** witch _____

59 godmother _____   **60** ewe _____

61 duchess _____   **62** lady _____

8

E 2

Copy each of these **phrases** making each **noun plural**. Don't forget to add the missing apostrophe.

63–64 the two car horn _____

65–66 the five girl jumper _____

67–68 the six bird beak _____

69–70 the four dog lead _____

8

E 2

Add a **suffix** to each of these words.

71 resource _____

72 shape _____

73 excite _____

74 woe _____

75 remote _____

76 false _____

77 tame _____

7

Choose an **adverb** to fill each gap. Each **adverb** may be used only once.

cheekily   wearily   lovingly   accidentally   wistfully   angrily   tunefully

78 Alice sang _____ tunefully.

79 Nina gently and _____ lovingly _____ washed and set her Gran's hair.

80 Manjit tripped and _____ accidentally _____ dropped the paint pot.

81 Jacob sighed _____ wearily _____ as he looked at the brand new sports car.

82 Sam _____ wearily _____ climbed into bed.

83 Tuhil yelled _____ angrily _____ at his dog as he chased a cat.

84 Anne _____ cheekily _____ chuckled.

Rewrite these sentences changing them from **plural** to **singular**.

85–86 The teams played their best.

_____

87–89 The cinemas in the area were showing the latest releases.

_____

90–92 The bonfires burnt for many hours.

_____

Copy the **proper nouns**, adding the missing capital letters.

93–100 february   bath rugby club   aberdeen

        sydney harbour   gangster   windsor castle

        contest   outcome   blue peter

        ben nevis   combination   alex roberts

_____   _____

_____   _____

_____   _____

_____   _____

It was not until the first week in November that replies from the Sticklebury penpals began to trickle into class. Oliver's letter from Simon was first to arrive.

Dear Oliver Boot,

You shouldn't have said in your letter that I might never grow out of my horrible habits because my mother read that bit by mistake, and my father had to give her a whisky to stop her crying.

How are you? I am very well. I have been sent to the ~~psi psyich pchi pci~~ psychologist because of the worse things that were private. So they aren't quite so private any more.

I tell terrible lies. It drives them mad, but I can't help it. I also run away from school. Quite often. But then I did them both at the same time, and that was a mistake. I ran away from school after morning assembly, and my next door neighbour pounced on me while I was half in and half out of the downstairs lavatory window, sneaking back in our house. I told her the school nurse sent me home because I had headlice, which was the only thing I could think of. But that evening the next door neighbour told Mum that I mustn't come round and play with her little Peter any more till I'd been sorted out. And Mum said: Sorted Out About What? And she said: About Headlice, Of Course. And then my mum went up the wall.

I begged her not to, with real tears in my eyes, but she wrote to the school nurse anyway, demanding an explanation and an apology. But I just happened to lose the letter inside a dustbin as I walked past it. I needn't have bothered, because Mum was so angry she phoned the school anyway. And when my teacher said: Simon, Where Is The Letter From Your Mother? I just panicked and told her my mother wasn't really my mother at all because I am a long lost, secret son of the Prince, and my mum and dad just pretend I am theirs to save the Queen from unbearable embarrassment.

So then my teacher said: Oh Yes? all sarcastically. And I panicked some more and said I could prove it with my handwriting. It is this bad because I am by nature left-handed, I said, and I am forced to write with my right hand to keep up my disguise.

All Right, my teacher said. Here Is A Pen, Simon. Write With Your Left Hand. So I asked: What Shall I Write? and she said tartly: How About This Is A Shocking Pack Of Lies? So I wrote with my left hand, and it was even worse than this, if you can imagine. And when I said it was simply because I hadn't had enough practice writing with my left hand, my teacher went right up the wall.

How are you? I hope you are quite well.
        Yours sincerely,
            Simon Huggett

From *A Pack of Liars* by Anne Fine

Underline the correct answers.

1 (Simon's, Oliver's, Peter's) letter was first to arrive.

2 Simon thinks he was sent to the psychologist because (he tells lies, he runs away from school, he has headlice).

3 Simon (did, didn't) have headlice.

Answer these questions.

4 What is meant by the line 'replies from the Sticklebury penpals began to trickle into class' (lines 1–2)?

_____

_____

_____

5 What does Simon mean when he says 'And then my mum went up the wall' (line 16)?

_____

_____

6 Why do you think Simon highlights the fact that he had 'real' tears (line 17)?

_____

_____

_____

7–8 In lines 18–19 Simon says 'But I just happened to lose the letter inside a dustbin as I walked past it.' What did Simon really do with the letter and why do you think he phrased it the way he did?

_____

_____

_____

9–10 Do you think Simon's left-handed argument is a valid one? What does it tell us about Simon's character?

_____

_____

_____

_____

Circle the words that either are or can be **nouns**.

11–17 herd   cheese   playful   booklet

      under   Richard   antelope   fracture

      hate   secure   questioned   similar

D 6

7

Add one of the **prefixes** to each word to make its **antonym**.

     non   im   ir   dis

D 9
E 2

18 _____responsible   19 _____existent

20 _____approve   21 _____balance

22 _____relevant   23 _____possible

24 _____charge   25 _____similar

8

Add the missing commas to these sentences.

D 4

26–27 Jess had to feed her cat give fresh water to the chickens take the dog for a walk and let the sheep out before school.

28–30 It was wet blustery sunny warm and windy during the Todd family walk.

31–33 Joseph spent his pocket money on a small pot of paint for his model aircraft a magazine a card for his mum's birthday a chocolate bar and a drink.

8

Write two **antonyms** for each of these words.

D 9

34–35 laugh   _____   _____

36–37 violent   _____   _____

38–39 small   _____   _____

6

Underline one **clause** (a section of a sentence with a **verb**) in each of these sentences.

D 2

40 Aimee wanted to go horse riding despite the pouring rain.

41 Nazar lost his coat at school on the coldest day of the year.

42 The snow fell heavily for many hours.

43 Dad stopped at the side of the road to answer his phone.

44 Helen ordered a cup of tea and an iced bun from the café on the high street.

45 Eleni worked hard at solving her maths problem despite her headache.

6

Add the **prefix** *sub* or *tele* to each of these words.

46	_____plot	47	_____standard
48	_____communications	49	_____normal
50	_____phone	51	_____merge
52	_____title	53	_____conscious

Write a more powerful **verb** for each of these verbs.

54	run	_____	55	laugh	_____
56	throw	_____	57	swallow	_____
58	wet	_____	59	speak	_____

Underline the **root word** for each of these words.

60	transatlantic	61	idleness	62	partnership
63	placement	64	non-toxic	65	unreal
66	dangerously	67	assessment	68	bicycle

Copy these sentences and write a **possessive pronoun** in place of the words in bold.

69–70 The apples on their side of the fence are **their apples** but those on our side are **our apples**.

_____

_____

71–72 **Your coat** is the same as **my coat**.

_____

73–74 **Kyle's bike** is bigger than **my bike**.

_____

75–76 **Jake's drink** tasted better than **Sarah's drink**.

_____

Add these **suffixes** to each word.

77 plan + ed = _____

78 admit + ing = _____

79 ballot + ed = _____

80 tax + ing = _____

81 equip + ed = _____

82 cancel + ed = _____

83 test + ed = _____

84 focus + ing = _____

85 enrol + ed = _____

86 hop + ing = _____

10

Add a different imperative **verb** to each of these sentences.

87 ___Wait___, there's a car coming!

88 _____, or we will be late.

89 _____, they're after us.

90 _____, in the name of the law!

91 _____ if you can't hear me at the back of the room.

92 _____ your percussion instruments.

93 _____ if you're happy!

7

Put these words in **alphabetical order**.

planet   pliable   platitude   pigment   plinth   placard   pleasure

94 (1) _____

95 (2) _____

96 (3) _____

97 (4) _____

98 (5) _____

99 (6) _____

100 (7) _____

7

Now go to the Progress Chart to record your score!   Total   **100**

Preparation for a marathon takes many months but at last it is **The Big Day**.

Depending on the time of the race, make sure you eat a small meal high in carbohydrate at least three hours beforehand. You may feel too nervous to eat, but you do need to top up your liver glycogen. Glycogen can only be stored in the liver for about 12 hours and is a necessary source of energy in the latter stages of the run. 5

If you are staying away from home the night before the race, take a selection of the breakfast you would usually eat with you as it's best not to introduce anything different at this late stage. Don't be persuaded to alter your habits, no matter how well-meaning your host may be.

Having worked out your route to the race, set out with plenty of time, aiming to get   10
there at least an hour before the start. Although you may find there is a very exciting atmosphere, try not to let it deflect you from your preparation. You can find yourself stopping and having chats and suddenly 20 minutes have gone by and you're not ready.

If you are with a club, they may supply transport and a safe place to store your kit, otherwise the organisers of the event will offer secure storage. Strip down to your   15
running kit, apply the plasters, store your kit then … queue for the loo! This is a crucial activity and at some events can take up to half an hour!

Cover up before the race with an old sweat-top or black bin-bag so as to keep warm. You can discard it when you get going.

Keep a small bottle of water with you, sipping from time to time, until about 20 minutes   20
before the start. You will be supplied with water on all races and some events will give you squash or a brand name replacement drink. Only use these if you are used to them in training, as they can upset your stomach. Some runners use energy bars and dried fruit to sustain their energy through the run; again, don't eat through the race if you're not used to it.

Set your own watch as you go over the start line, as it can be up to 10 minutes   25
after the actual start gun, depending on the attendance at the race. That way you can monitor your own race.

Aim to run the first five miles at your predicted race speed. Being suddenly surrounded by a variety of runners can throw you off, so run your own race and don't worry about the rest.   30

You're off …
Enjoy the race!

From Marathon Manual *by Cathy Shipton with Liz McColgan*

Underline the correct answers.

1 You should finally eat (just before, three hours before, twelve hours before) the start of the race.

2 Why is it important to top up your glycogen levels before the race?

(it stops you feeling nervous, it tops up your energy levels, it allows you to skip breakfast)

3 Why can it sometimes take many minutes from the start of the race for the runner to actually cross the start line?

(because the runner isn't prepared, because there are many runners wanting to cross the start line, because some runners like to start the race by walking)

3

Answer these questions.

4 Why might the runner stay away from home the night before a race?

_____

5–6 Give two reasons why it is important to arrive approximately an hour before the race starts.

_____

_____

_____

7 Why does the author describe going to the loo as a 'crucial activity' (lines 16–17)?

_____

_____

8 What is the meaning of the word 'sustain' on line 24?

_____

9–10 Give two reasons why the use of a bin-bag or sweat-top is suggested.

_____

_____

_____

7

Add the missing *ie* or *ei* letters to complete each word correctly.

11 h_____r

12 d_____

13 fr_____ght

14 v_____w

15 f_____nt

16 y_____ld

17 n_____ghbours

18 s_____ze

19 conc_____ted

E 2

9

Rewrite each sentence as if you are writing about yourself.

D 6

20 She enjoys swimming. _____

21 They made their favourite cakes. _____

22 He loves playing football. _____

23 The teacher stopped her on the way to class.

_____

4

Write an **antonym** for each of these words.

D 9

24 high _____

25 cold _____

26 over _____

27 legal _____

28 difficult _____

29 mobile _____

6

Add different **adverbs** to complete each sentence.

D 6

30–31 The children walked _____ home from school and talked to Mum

_____.

32–33 The children walked_____ home from school and talked to Mum

_____.

34–35 The children walked _____ home from school and talked to Mum

_____.

36–37 The children walked _____ home from school and talked to Mum

_____.

8

Add the missing commas to these sentences.

D 4

38 Fed up because the computer continually broke down they decided to buy a new one.

39 The sunbathers lay on the beach all afternoon unaware of how burnt they were becoming.

40–41 The stranger a well-dressed man joined the party.

42 In Madagascar the inner skins of leaves are peeled and then stretched out in the tropical sun which dries and bleaches them.

43 While Henry was swimming at his local pool the lights suddenly went off.

44 When it was announced that the fancy-dress competition was about to take place we huddled together to plan our escape.

7
E 2

Write each of these words in its **plural** form.

45 punch　＿＿＿＿＿＿＿　　**46** bus　＿＿＿＿＿＿＿

47 sausage　＿＿＿＿＿＿＿　　**48** convoy　＿＿＿＿＿＿＿

49 dress　＿＿＿＿＿＿＿　　**50** waltz　＿＿＿＿＿＿＿

51 tariff　＿＿＿＿＿＿＿　　**52** thief　＿＿＿＿＿＿＿

8
D 6

Underline the **nouns** in this poem.

53–60　Daisy, Daisy,　　　　　　　For I can't afford a carriage –

　　　　Give me your answer do,　　But you'll look sweet

　　　　I'm half crazy　　　　　　Upon the seat

　　　　All for the love of you;　　Of a bicycle made for two!

　　　　It won't be a stylish marriage,　　　　　　　　　Anon.

8
D 5

Rewrite these sentences and add the missing speech marks.

61–64 What do we do now? grumbled Jay through gritted teeth. They're bound to sabotage our camp.

They can't do anything until it gets dark, consoled Mimi. We'll just have to make sure we stay up all through the night.

＿＿＿＿＿＿＿＿＿＿＿＿＿＿＿＿＿＿＿＿＿＿＿＿＿＿＿＿＿＿

＿＿＿＿＿＿＿＿＿＿＿＿＿＿＿＿＿＿＿＿＿＿＿＿＿＿＿＿＿＿

＿＿＿＿＿＿＿＿＿＿＿＿＿＿＿＿＿＿＿＿＿＿＿＿＿＿＿＿＿＿

＿＿＿＿＿＿＿＿＿＿＿＿＿＿＿＿＿＿＿＿＿＿＿＿＿＿＿＿＿＿

65–68 I'm frozen, complained Jay. It really is cold and dark, he sighed. Maybe they aren't going to come back tonight.

Mimi considered Jay's comment. But maybe they will! she replied.

_____

_____

_____

_____

Write one word for each **definition**. Each word begins with G.

69 A hard, transparent substance that is easily broken.   _____

70 A Roman man who was forced to fight for public amusement.   _____

71 A movement that conveys a meaning.   _____

72 A sphere showing the map of the world.   _____

73 A valuable, yellow metal.   _____

74 A small, flying insect that can bite people.   _____

75 A slope.   _____

76 Another name for rubbish.   _____

Underline the correct **homophone** in each bracket.

77–78 The (boy, buoy) untied his boat from the (boy, buoy).

79–80 The (fair, fare) for a ride at the (fair, fare) was £3.00.

81–82 Jason (new, knew) his (new, knew) jeans would fit perfectly.

83–84 'Are you (sure/shore) we can see the (sure/shore) from here?' asked the children.

85–86 The (ewe, yew) died after eating the (ewe, yew), a very poisonous plant.

Underline the **reported speech** sentences only and write them again as direct speech.

87–94 Kate's dad called to her to hurry up.

'What's the time?' the teacher asked.

'Let's go to the playground,' pleaded the twins.

Sarah explained to Pete she was going on holiday soon.

The Singh family yelled to the passing boat that they needed help.

'Quick! The match starts in 10 minutes,' called Joel.

Mum asked her friend if she thought it might rain today.

'Have you found a snail yet?' queried Aimee.

_____

_____

_____

_____

8

D 8

Write the **diminutive** for each of these.

95 pig   _____   **96** book   _____

97 duck   _____   **98** hill   _____

99 owl   _____   **100** statue   _____

6

Now go to the Progress Chart to record your score!   Total   100

Paper 4

'This is Lord Fauntleroy, Mrs Mellon,' he said. 'Lord Fauntleroy, this is Mrs Mellon, who is the housekeeper.'

Cedric gave her his hand, his eyes lighting up.

'Was it you who sent the cat?' he said. 'I'm much obliged to you ma'am.'

Mrs Mellon's handsome old face looked as pleased as the face of the lodge-keeper's   5
wife had done.

'I should know his lordship anywhere,' she said to Mr Havisham. 'He has the Captain's face and way. It's a great day, this, sir.'

Cedric wondered why it was a great day. He looked at Mrs Mellon curiously. It seemed to him for a moment as if there were tears in her eyes, and yet it was   10
evident she was not unhappy. She smiled down at him.

'The cat left two beautiful kittens here,' she said. 'They shall be sent up to your lordship's nursery.'

Mr Havisham said a few words to her in a low voice.

'In the library, sir,' Mrs Mellon replied. 'His lordship is to be taken there alone.'   15

A few minutes later the very tall footman in livery, who had escorted Cedric to the library door, opened it and announced: 'Lord Fauntleroy, my lord,' in quite a majestic tone. If he was only a footman, he felt it was rather a grand occasion when the heir came home to his own land and possessions, and was ushered into the presence of the old Earl, whose place and title he was to take.   20

Cedric crossed the threshold into the room. It was a very large and splendid room, with massive carven furniture in it, and shelves upon shelves of books … For a moment Cedric thought there was nobody in the room, but soon he saw that by the fire burning on the wide hearth there was a large easy chair, and that in that chair someone was sitting – someone who did not at first turn to look at him.

But he had attracted attention in one quarter at least. On the floor, by the armchair, lay a dog, a huge tawny mastiff with body and limbs almost as big as a lion's; and this great creature rose majestically and slowly, and marched towards the little fellow with a heavy step.

Then the person in the chair spoke. 'Dougal,' he called, 'come back, sir.' …

Cedric put his hand on the big dog's collar in the most natural way in the world, and they strayed forward together, Dougal sniffing as he went.

And then the Earl looked up …

… Cedric looked at him just as he had looked at the woman at the lodge and at the housekeeper, and came quite close to him.

'Are you the Earl?' he said. 'I'm your grandson, you know, that Mr Havisham brought. I'm Lord Fauntleroy.'

He held out his hand because he thought it must be the polite and proper thing to do even with earls. 'I hope you are very well,' he continued, with the utmost friendliness. 'I'm very glad to see you.'

The Earl shook hands with him, with a curious gleam in his eyes; just at first he was so astonished that he scarcely knew what to say. He stared at the picturesque little apparition from under his shaggy brows, and took it all in from head to foot.

'Glad to see me, are you?' he said.

From *Little Lord Fauntleroy* by Frances Hodgson Burnett

Underline the correct answers.

1 Lord Fauntleroy's first name is (Mr Havisham, Dougal, Cedric).

2 Mrs Mellon had tears in her eyes because she (had dust in them, was sad, was happy).

3 On line 43 the Earl is described as having 'shaggy brows'. They are a description of his (fringe, eyebrows, an item of clothing).

Answer these questions.

4 What piece of evidence in the passage suggests that Mrs Mellon had been housekeeper for the Earl for many years?

_____

_____

5 Why was it a 'great day' (line 8)?

_____

_____

6 Explain why when speaking to Mrs Mellon, Mr Havisham did so 'in a low voice' (line 14).

_____

_____

7 Explain in your own words what is meant by the sentence 'But he had attracted attention in one quarter at least' (line 26).

_____

_____

8–9 Find two pieces of evidence that suggest this passage was written many years ago.

_____

_____

_____

10 Why do you think the Earl 'scarcely knew what to say' (line 42) on meeting Little Lord Fauntleroy?

_____

_____

7

D 6

Underline the correct form of the **verb** to complete each sentence.

11 The dogs race/races after the ball.

12 Ben stir/stirs the cake mixture.

13 The chick learns to scratch/scratches the earth.

14 The Head Teacher sing/sings loudly and clearly during assembly.

15 The rain pour/pours down on the washing hung on the line.

16 Rashid peel/peels a banana.

17 The duck feed/feeds greedily on the bread.

7

Extend each of these words into a different **compound word**.

D 11

18 table_____   19 table_____

20 any_____   21 any_____

22 snow_____   23 snow_____

24 hand_____   25 hand_____

26 some_____   27 some_____

10

D 6

Add a different **adjective** in each gap to complete the sentences.

28 All the children liked the _____ classroom.

29 The _____ spoon was used for cake-making.

30 George didn't like his _____ teacher.

31 The _____ chickens scratched in the vegetable garden.

32 Eva's _____ computer made researching her homework much easier.

33 The Asser family excitedly headed towards the _____ circus.

6

E 2

Write a word to match each clue. Each word ends in a vowel.

34 A small wind instrument   _____

35 A mountain with a crater   _____

36 A folding frame covered with fabric which opens to give protection

_____

37 A liquid for washing hair   _____

38 Tiny pieces of coloured paper, often thrown over newlyweds _____

39 A flat round of dough covered with a savoury mixture _____

6

40–45 Write a short argument between two car drivers who nearly crashed, that includes at least two full-stops, two question marks and two exclamation marks.

D 1
D 5

_____

_____

_____

_____

_____

_____

6

With a line, match the words with the same key spelling patterns.

E 2

46 experience	balance
47 thorough	agent
48 performance	optician
49 plumber	borough
50 entrant	licence
51 present	instant
52 electrician	numbness

7

Write whether each of these sentences is in the **past**, **present** or **future tense**.

D 6

53 I walked home. _____

54 I am going to buy lunch. _____

55 I wrote an exciting story. _____

56 I am sipping my soup carefully. _____

57 I have made some cakes. _____

58 I will tidy my bedroom. _____

59 I am typing at my computer. _____

7

Write each of these words adding the **suffix** *ful* correctly.

E 2

60 thought _____   **61** awe   _____

62 pity   _____   **63** deceit   _____

64 shame   _____   **65** mercy   _____

66 hope   _____   **67** dread   _____

8

D 2

Complete each sentence by adding a different **conjunction**.

68 I still went swimming _____ I had a bad cold.

69 Laurel chose to go to Horseworld for her birthday treat _____ she loves horses.

70 Mum bought me some new trainers _____ I could run faster!

71 Niall wanted to go out on his bike _____ it was raining.

72 Wusai missed a day off school _____ so did Gina.

73 Jacob has been able to use a knife and fork _____ he was three.

74 Dan's new puppy couldn't go for a walk _____ he had all his injections.

75 We left the swimming pool _____ it was closing.

8

C 4

Write which animal these **onomatopoeic** words remind you of.

76 roar   _____   **77** baa   _____

78 grunt   _____   **79** gobble   _____

80 mew   _____   **81** cluck   _____

82 woof   _____

7

D 6

Underline the **pronouns** in the sentences.

83–84 We must buy him a packet as well.

85–87 Where is mine? Have you got it?

88–89 His is longer than yours.

90 Why are theirs the same?

91–92 I wonder what they are doing.

10

Rewrite these words adding the **suffix** *ing* to each one.

93 make _____   94 wake _____

95 heal _____   96 vex _____

97 hope _____   98 enrol _____

99 argue _____   100 tie _____

8

Now go to the Progress Chart to record your score! Total ◯ 100

Paper 5

Water in Our World

Three-quarters of Earth's surface is covered by water and
nearly all of it is contained in the oceans and seas.
The rest, a very small amount, is in the air or froze long ago
to form polar ice caps. Most of the water we use comes from
rivers and lakes, or water that has seeped through rocks and collected underground.   *5*

- The movement of water between the land, the sea and the air is called the water
  cycle. As the Sun heats the water in the oceans, rivers, lakes and plants, some of
  the water evaporates, which means that it changes into water vapour (a gas) and
  rises into the air. High in the sky, the water vapour cools and changes back into tiny
  drops of liquid water. This process is called condensation. The water drops   *10*
  gather together to make clouds and eventually fall as rain, hail or snow. The cycle
  then starts all over again. As a result of this recycling, the amount of water on Earth
  always remains the same.

- About 97 per cent of all water is the salty water of the oceans and seas. The sea is
  salty because salts are either washed off the land by rivers or escape from   *15*
  cracks in the ocean floor. Other salts come from undersea volcanoes.

- Water makes up the greatest part of the bodies of plants and animals and is vital
  for all life. Did you know that your body is made up of more than 70 per cent water?
  You need to take in about two litres of water a day, and much more when it is hot or
  you are working hard. Aquatic animals live surrounded by water, but those that   *20*
  live on land have to find water or get all that they need from their food.

- Sea water has no colour, but appears blue or green because both blue and
  green light from the Sun reach deeper below the surface of the water than
  other colours. The sea also reflects the colour of the sky and changes in the
  weather.   *25*

From *Questions and Answers: Oceans and Rivers* by Barbara Taylor

Underline the correct answers.

1 What is the Earth's surface mainly covered in?

(land, water, land and water equally)

2 What percentage of water on Earth is salty?

(3%, 70%, 97%)

3 What colour is sea water?

(blue, green, clear)

Answer these questions.

4 Why is condensation described as a 'recycling' process (line 12)?

_____

_____

_____

_____

5 What does the word 'reflects' mean (line 24)?

_____

_____

6–7 Give two reasons why the sea is salty.

_____

_____

_____

_____

8–9 Read this sentence: *If people don't get enough water from eating and drinking they may become dehydrated.* In which bullet point would this sentence best fit and why?

_____

_____

10 Look again at the third bullet point. Write a subheading in the form of a question for this paragraph.

_____

_____

7

Circle the **preposition** (a word that relates other words to each other) in each of these sentences.

D 6

11 Gran slept for hours in the armchair.

12 Jay jumped behind the leather sofa.

13 Caroline walked carefully among the bluebells.

14 Yousef climbed up the cliff wall.

15 The twins looked through the letterbox to see if anyone was home.

16 The electrician slipped down the ladder and broke his leg.

17–18 Mum placed the drinks on the tray before carrying them up the stairs.

8

Write the short form often used for each of these words.

D 10

19 aeroplane _____ **20** handkerchief _____

21 head-teacher _____ **22** newspaper _____

23 champion _____ **24** examination _____

6

Underline the **verbs** in each of these sentences.

D 6

25 Don't grab at my clothes!

26–27 Jump down and sprint!

28 Wait for me!

29 Don't surprise me like that!

30–31 Run, they're catching us!

7

Write a **synonym** for each of the words in bold.

D 9

32 The captured soldiers were **interrogated**. _____

33 Mum complained about the **racket** my music made. _____

34 I was surprised that such a famous person looked so **ordinary**.

_____

35 Dave was given the **option** to go ice-skating or to the cinema.

_____

36 The Captain **reviewed** his troops.   _____

37 The rope around their wrists was **taut**.   _____

38 That's **wonderful** news!   _____

7

Rewrite these sentences, adding the missing punctuation.

D 4
D 5

39–42 What time does the party start Helen called

_____

_____

43–49 We must concentrate said David If we don't get this work done we'll have to miss our playtime

_____

_____

11

Match to each of these words a word with the same letter string but a different sound.

E 2

stove   height   barn   head   glove   plead

50 weight   _____

51 earn   _____

52 love   _____

53 bead   _____

54 drove   _____

55 dead   _____

6

Rewrite these sentences without the double negatives.

D 13

56 Jake hasn't walked no half-marathon.

_____

57 There wasn't no milk left by the milkman.

_____

58 Cath hasn't no drink for her lunch.

_____

59 Dad's not never going there again.

_____

60 There aren't no red squirrels here.

_____

61 I don't not have enough money to buy that.

_____

6

Write a **homophone** for each of these words.

E 2

62 site _____	**63** boarder _____
64 horse _____	**65** stationary _____
66 flower _____	**67** shore _____
68 wave _____	**69** sundae _____

8

Add a powerful **verb** in the gaps to make each sentence interesting.

D 6

70–71 The dog _____ towards the sea and _____ into it.

72–73 The plane _____ and the passengers _____.

74–75 '_____ or we'll never win the relay race!' _____ the team.

76–77 The children _____ through the snow until they could see the

_____ lights.

78–79 As the queen _____ the crowd _____.

10

Put these counties in **alphabetical order**.

Northumberland   Somerset   Suffolk   Norfolk
South Glamorgan   Nottinghamshire   Strathclyde

80 (1) _____   **81** (2) _____

82 (3) _____   **83** (4) _____

84 (5) _____   **85** (6) _____

86 (7) _____

Underline the **connectives** (word or words that join clauses or sentences) in each sentence.

87 Ella had to sit down for tea even though her favourite programme was on.

88 Daniel needed his boots but he couldn't find them.

89 The runner had hurt his ankle, nevertheless he still started the race.

90 Veejay handed in his homework although it was past the deadline.

91 The kittens drank their milk and chased the ball before settling down for the night.

92 It was time for Jane to go home though she wanted to stay longer.

Circle the words which have a soft G.

93–100 knowledge   gaggle   garage   imagine   gourd   refugee   generous

governor   dungeon   gradient   gigantic   grime   message   wrong   frog

Now go to the Progress Chart to record your score!   Total   100

When the end of the war did come, it came swiftly, almost unexpectedly it seemed
to the men around me. There was little joy, little celebration of victory, only a sense
of profound relief that at last it was finished and done with. Albert left the happy
cluster of men gathered together in the yard that cold November morning and
strolled over to talk to me. 'Five minutes time and it'll be finished, Joey, all over.   *5*
Jerry's had about enough of it, and so have we. No one really wants to go on any
more. At eleven o'clock the guns will stop and then that will be that. Only wish that
David could have been here to see it.'

Since David's death Albert had not been himself. I had not once seen him smile
or joke, and he often fell into prolonged brooding silences when he was with me.   *10*
There was no more singing, no more whistling. I tried all that I could to comfort him,
resting my head on his shoulder and nickering gently to him, but he seemed quite
inconsolable. Even the news that the war was finally ending brought no light back
to his eyes. The bell in the clock tower over the gateway rang out eleven times, and
the men shook each other solemnly by the hand or clapped each other on the back   *15*
before returning to the stables.

The fruits of victory were to prove bitter indeed for me, but to begin with the end
of the war changed little. The Veterinary Hospital operated as it always had done,
and the flow of sick and injured horses seemed rather to increase than to diminish.
From the yard gate we saw the unending columns of fighting men marching jauntily   *20*
back to the railway stations, and we looked on as the tanks and guns and wagons
rolled by on their way home. But we were left where we were. Like the other men,
Albert was becoming impatient. Like them he wanted only to get home as quickly
as possible.

Morning parade took place as usual every morning in the centre of the cobbled   *25*
yard, followed by Major Martin's inspection of the horses and stables. But one
dreary, drizzling morning, with the wet cobbles shining grey in the early morning
light, Major Martin did not inspect the stables as usual. Sergeant 'Thunder' stood
the men at ease and Major Martin announced the re-embarkation plans for the unit.
He was finishing his short speech: 'So we shall be at Victoria Station by six o'clock   *30*
on Saturday evening – with any luck. Chances are you'll be home by Christmas.'

'Permission to speak, sir?' Sergeant 'Thunder' ventured.

'Carry on, Sergeant.'

'It's about the 'orses, sir,' Sergeant 'Thunder' said. 'I think the men would like to
know what's going to 'appen with the 'orses. Will they be with us on the same ship,   *35*
sir? Or will they be coming along later?'

Major Martin shifted his feet and looked down at his boots. He spoke softly as he
did not want to be heard. 'No, Sergeant,' he said. 'I'm afraid the horses won't be
coming with us at all.'

From *War Horse* by Michael Morpurgo

Underline the correct answers.

1 In which month did the war end?

(October, November, December)

2 Who is Joey?

(a soldier friend of Albert's, a wounded soldier, a horse)

○ 2

Answer these questions.

3 Why had Albert 'not been himself' (line 9)?

_____

4 What was the significance of the bell at the gateway ringing out eleven times?

_____

_____

5 Write another word the author could have used instead of 'nickering' (line 12).

_____

6–7 Give the meaning of the following words as they are used in the passage:

profound (line 3) _____

jauntily (line 20) _____

8–9 Using evidence from the passage, describe how you think war has affected Albert.

_____

_____

_____

_____

10 In lines 37–38 the sergeant 'spoke softly as he did not want to be heard'. Why?

_____

_____

_____

○ 8

Write the **collective noun** for each of these living creatures.

D 6

11 elephants _____ **12** sheep _____

13 kittens _____ **14** ants _____

15 fish _____ **16** lions _____

17 bees _____

○ 7

Write a second **clause** to extend each of these sentences.

18 Rupa grabbed her coat _____

_____

19 The school coaches arrived at Raglan Castle _____

_____

20 The shot rang out around the stadium _____

_____

21 Joe had planned every detail of the surprise _____

_____

22 Poppy copied Tom's answers _____

_____

23 The cat pounced _____

_____

24 Dan felt trapped _____

_____

7

Add *ory*, *ery* or *ary* to each of these words.

25 Febru_____

26 diction_____

27 hist_____

28 myst_____

29 ordin_____

30 secret_____

31 jewell_____

32 necess_____

33 mem_____

9

Add the missing apostrophe or apostrophes to each sentence.

34 Dont go over there!

35 We couldve gone to the beach.

36 Theyll be home soon.

37–38 Its time to go to ballet, isnt it?

39 I shant eat my tea!

40 Well buy some sweets tomorrow.

7

31

Complete each of these expressions using the words below.

bush   cart   apple   ghost   head   rat   heart

41 Don't give up the _____.

42 To smell a _____.

43 To hang your _____ in shame.

44 To put the _____ before the horse.

45 Absence makes the _____ grow fonder.

46 Don't beat about the _____.

47 An _____ a day keeps the doctor away.

7

Rewrite these book titles, adding the missing capital letters.

48–50 classic children's stories

_____

51–54 the little book of facts

_____

55–58 keeping ponies season by season

_____

11

D 6

Circle the word which is …

59 a **verb**	bus	happily	bounce	it
60 a **pronoun**	they	ran	through	rain
61 a **noun**	tree	but	pretty	before
62 an **adverb**	gate	new	kicked	greedily
63 a **preposition**	under	marmalade	we	you
64 an **adjective**	jacket	lank	love	swarm
65 a **conjunction**	hidden	giant	cold	although

7

Rewrite these sentences in the **past tense**.

D 6

66 I'm going swimming.

_____

67 The thunder is frightening.

_____

68 The children are going to pick blackberries.

_____

69 My gran is living on her own.

_____

70 The dog is swimming in the pond.

_____

71 The school orchestra are practising.

_____

6

Underline the four words or terms that have entered our language in the last fifty years.

E 2

72–75 Internet   website   automobile   television   email   electricity   telephone   CD

4

Underline one word in each group which is not a **synonym** for the rest.

D 9

76	respond	acknowledge	ignore	answer	reply
77	charm	cheer	amuse	annoy	delight
78	reassure	worry	agonise	upset	unsettle
79	ask	investigate	quiz	examine	reply

4

Finish each sentence by adding a helper **verb** to match the **tense** in bold.

D 6

80 The horse _____ racing towards the sea.   **past**

81 The pigs _____ guzzling down their swill.   **present**

82 The jewels _____ discovered by the thieves.   **present**

83 James _____ running in the relay race.   **present**

84 The telephone _____ ringing.   **past**

85 Fern's class _____ going to read to the younger children.   **past**

6

Circle the words which have a soft *C*.

86–92 innocent   centimetre   collapse   electricity   catch   sequence

         clueless   ache   practice   synchronise   fantastic   peace

         condense   fancy   alcove

Underline the **root word** of each of these words.

93 agreeable   **94** direction   **95** forceful

96 mismatch   **97** optional   **98** reloading

99 discoloured   **100** tiresome

Now go to the Progress Chart to record your score!   Total   100

Paper 7

Lucy Gray; or, Solitude

Oft I had heard of Lucy Gray:
And, when I crossed the wild,
I chanced to see at break of day
The solitary child.

No mate, no comrade Lucy knew;   5
She dwelt on a wide moor,
– The sweetest thing that ever grew
Beside a human door!

You yet may spy the fawn at play,
The hare upon the green;   10
But the sweet face of Lucy Gray
Will never more be seen.

'To-night will be a stormy night –
You to the town must go;
And take a lantern, Child, to light   15
Your mother through the snow.'

'That, Father! will I gladly do:
'Tis scarcely afternoon –
The minster-clock has just struck two,
And yonder is the moon!'   20

At this the Father raised his hook,
And snapped a faggot-band;
He plied his work; – and Lucy took
The lantern in her hand.

Not blither is the mountain roe: 25
With many a wanton stroke
Her feet disperse the powdery snow,
That rises up like smoke.

The storm came on before its time:
She wandered up and down;   30
And many a hill did Lucy climb:
But never reached the town.

The wretched parents all that night
Went shouting far and wide;
But there was neither sound nor sight   35
To serve them for a guide.

At day-break on a hill they stood
They overlooked the moor;
And thence they saw the bridge of wood,
A furlong from their door.   40

They wept – and, turning homeward, cried,
'In heaven we all shall meet;'
– When in the snow the mother spied
The print of Lucy's feet.

Then downwards from the steep hill's edge   *45*
They tracked the footmarks small;
And through the broken hawthorn hedge,
And by the long-stone wall;

And then an open field they crossed:
The marks were still the same;   *50*
They tracked them on, nor ever lost;
And to the bridge they came.

They followed from the snowy bank
Those footmarks, one by one,
Into the middle of the plank;   *55*
And further there were none!

– Yet some maintain that to this day
She is a living child;
That you may see sweet Lucy Gray
Upon the lonesome wild.   *60*

O'er rough and smooth she trips along,
And never looks behind;
And sings a solitary song
That whistles in the wind.

William Wordsworth

Underline the correct answers.

1 In which season was this poem set?

(summer, autumn, <u>winter</u>)

2 Why was Lucy sent to meet her mother?

(<u>to guide her home with a light</u>, to keep her company on her walk home, to ask
her to buy a light before the storm)

3 Did Lucy make it to town before the storm?

(yes, <u>no</u>)

Answer these questions.

4 Why did Lucy's father feel it was safe to send her to town?

_____

_____

5–6 Find two lines in the poem that show Lucy had walked a long way.

_____

_____

_____

7–8 How do you think Lucy's parents felt once they discovered she was missing? Use evidence from the poem to support your answer.

_____

_____

_____

_____

9–10 What evidence is there that this poem was written a long time ago?

_____

_____

_____

Write *there*, *their* or *they're* in each of the gaps.

11 The Jacob family were on _____ way home.

12–13 _____ all very tired after _____ late night.

14–15 The chocolate biscuits are _____ but remember _____ for everyone!

Write *to*, *too* or *two* in each of the gaps.

16–17 Dad had _____ walk _____ the station this morning.

18–19 Dave has had _____ days off school and he is not _____ well again today.

20 Mum is going to buy some dog food but I need to remind her she needs some cat food _____.

Underline the **adjectival phrase** in each sentence.

21 Freda, the long-haired, cream-coloured cat, slept soundly.

22 Florence loved her thick, long, dark hair.

23 Jim dived through the sticky, wet mud, saving the goal.

7

E 2

5

E 2

5

D 2

24 The friends burnt while playing in the blistering, scorching heat of the sun.

25 The baby-sitter told exciting, but scary and often terrifying, late night stories!

26 The glistening, coloured vase shimmered in the sunlight.

6

With a line, match the rhyming slang phrases with their meaning.

27 skin and blister   feet

28 apples and pears   knees

29 bread and cheese   sister

30 plates of meat   road

31 sugar and honey   stairs

32 frog and toad   money

6
D 9

Write a **synonym** for each of these words.

33 humorous _____   34 modify _____

35 monotonous _____   36 camouflage _____

37 stagger _____   38 wrench _____

39 unfamiliar _____   40 vandalise _____

8

Copy the passage, adding the missing capital letters and punctuation.

D 1
D 6
D 5

41–58 listen everyone I have an announcement to make shouted mr bridges above the noise

ive arranged for us all to camp out at harlington hall we will see for ourselves if it is haunted or not

the colour faded from Hannahs face

_____

_____

_____

_____

_____

_____

18

Write each of these words in its **plural form**.

59 army   _____   60 quantity   _____

61 trolley   _____   62 cowboy   _____

63 novelty   _____   64 responsibility   _____

65 stairway   _____   66 remedy   _____

Write the **abbreviations** of these words.

67 Criminal Investigation Department   _____

68 kilometres   _____

69 do it yourself   _____

70 United Nations   _____

71 unidentified flying object   _____

72 very important person   _____

73 for example   _____

Complete each sentence with a different **adverb**.

74 Jack screamed _____.

75 They crawled _____.

76 I smiled _____.

77 Meena danced _____.

78 We played _____.

79 Sam wrote _____.

Rewrite these sentences as **reported speech**.

80 Sarah enquired, 'What time shall we meet?'

_____

81 'It must be lunchtime!' exclaimed a hungry boy.

_____

82 'I wish I didn't have so much work to do,' Tony moaned.

_____

83 The park keeper called out, 'Dogs aren't allowed in this park!'

_____

84 'Clear up your room!' shouted Mum.

_____

85 Jane asked, 'Have you checked out this website?'

_____

6

Add the **suffix** to each of these words. Don't forget spelling changes.

86 sore + ness = _____

87 regard + less = _____

88 plenty + ful = _____

89 achieve + ment = _____

90 examine + tion = _____

91 shape + less = _____

92 stress + ful = _____

93 tire + some = _____

8

In each gap add a different **connective**.

94 The soldiers continued to fight _____ they were exhausted.

95 The children finally arrived at the campsite _____ they could set up their tents.

96 George telephoned his Grandad _____ he'd heard he wasn't well.

97 Wang Ling wanted to go out to play _____ she had to finish her story first.

98 Mark was pleased it was football practice _____ it was his favourite sport.

99 Class 6 were cooking _____ they heard the fire alarm.

100 Gaby lost the trainers _____ were the most comfortable to wear.

7

Now go to the Progress Chart to record your score! Total 100

Paper 8

Thinking of sponsoring a child?

Read how for just a small monthly amount you can help bring health and opportunities to children in poor communities.

Every child has potential

There are 600 million children who live on less than 70p a day – that's ten times   5
the UK population.

In Africa, Latin America and large areas of Asia, acute poverty is depriving children of good health. Many children are suffering from avoidable infections or diseases spread through contaminated water.

Trung wants to read An education would be the best start Trung could have in life.   10
But the nearest school is 20 miles away.

Mamadou's family needs seeds Mamadou and his family have a field that could provide food for them but they need seeds, plus advice to help them work their land more effectively.

Amina needs clean water Amina's village only has access to dirty water, so many   15
children's lives are threatened by waterborne illnesses such as dysentery and diarrhoea.

As a sponsor, you can help more children realise that potential

When we begin working with a community, the first thing we do is talk to community leaders, parents and the children themselves to find out what they need most.

It could be access to clean water, a school for both boys and girls, a medical centre   20
or an income-generating scheme so that families can earn a living.

Children represent the future and we believe sponsorship is the best way to help communities. It is children like Trung, Mamadou and Amina who will be able to pass on their knowledge and skills to the next generation.

Taken from a Plan leaflet on sponsoring a child

Underline the correct answers.

   1 How many children live on less than 70p a day?

      (1 million, 10 million, 600 million)

   2 What is this leaflet asking for?

      (teachers to help educate children, people to talk with village leaders, money each month to support their work)

Answer these questions.

3–4 How does the money provided by the sponsors help the children who need it? Give one example.

_____

_____

_____

5 Who do the charity workers talk to when they first identify a community that needs help?

_____

_____

6 What is meant by 'an income-generating scheme' (line 21)?

_____

_____

7 What is the meaning of the word 'contaminated' on line 9?

_____

8 What is meant by the heading 'Every child has potential' (line 4)?

_____

_____

9–10 Describe two ways the information presented in the leaflet is used to encourage people to become sponsors.

_____

_____

_____

_____

8

Add the **suffix** to each word. Make any necessary spelling changes.

E 2

11 instal + ing = _____

12 label + ed = _____

13 quarrel + some = _____

14 whinge + ing = _____

15 collapse + ible = _____

16 marvel + ous = _____

17 fulfil + ment = _____

18 shovel + ful = _____

8

Add the missing commas to these sentences.

D 4

19–20 The coat lining felt odd sort of lumpy and I thought I could hear a faint squeak coming from inside it.

21 As it came nearer it slowly took on the form of a boat.

22 A dreaded monster lived in the castle nearby watching over the townsfolk's every move.

23 Rick and James began to argue each blaming the other for the broken window.

24 You know what it is like you try to work but you find yourself staring out the window.

25–26 Sam who was hungry after playing football was glad to see his mum making sandwiches.

8

Write the masculine form of each of these words.

D 8

27 nanny-goat _____

28 heroine _____

29 countess _____

30 goose _____

31 doe _____

32 niece _____

6

Underline the **adverbs** in the following passage.

D 6

33–39 Henry rushed quickly home after finishing school. He waited impatiently as his mum hurriedly finished her phone conversation.
'Mum, Mum, I've been chosen to narrate the school play,' he said excitedly.
'Mrs Smith says I must work diligently at learning the lines so they can start rehearsals as soon as possible.'
'Well done! I always knew you'd get a part in the play but narrator is undeniably a hard role. You'll have to read through the lines constantly so you know them inside out,' said Mum.

7

Write two **antonyms** for each word.

40–41 hate _____ _____

42–43 walk _____ _____

44–45 huge _____ _____

46–47 windy _____ _____

48–49 light _____ _____

Add the missing vowels to each of these words.

50 c___nf___tt___   51 v___lc___n___   52 sp___gh___tt___

53 sh___mp___ ___   54 umbr___ll___   55 c___ll___

Complete the table below.

56–64

	er	**est**	**ish**
large			
sweet			
cold			

Write a different **preposition** in each gap.

65 Leo hid _____ his bedding.

66 Poppy climbed _____ the hay bales.

67 The sheepdog jumped _____ the gate.

68–69 The train went _____ the tunnel then _____ the sea wall.

70 The teacher walked _____ the playground.

71 Dev snuggled _____ his duvet to keep warm.

Rewrite these sentences and add the missing punctuation.

D 4
D 5

72–75 It's time we set off on holiday called Mum

_____

76–82 Where is my coat shouted Danny it is too cold to go outside without it

_____

_____

11

With a line, match the word to the country from where you think it is borrowed.

E 2

83 ballet   Germany

84 karate   France

85 dachshund   Japan

86 bravo   Italy

4

Rewrite each sentence as though you are writing about someone else.

D 6

87 I fainted with the pain. _____

88 I eat quickly.   _____

89 I fell down the stairs.   _____

90 We love playing computer games.

_____

91 I'm walking the dog.   _____

92 We're going to see a film.

_____

6

Underline the correct word in brackets.

D 6

93–94 It (was, were) time to go to bed but they (was, were) not tired.

95 What (is, are) Dad going to do about the broken door?

96 When (is, are) the spring bulbs going to appear?

97 The phone rang when we (was, were) outside.

98–99 The volcano (is, are) erupting as the villagers (is, are) sleeping.

100 When (is, are) we going swimming?

8

Now go to the Progress Chart to record your score!   Total   100

'At last!' said Eustace as he came slithering down a slide of loose stones (*scree*, they call it) and found himself on the level. 'And now, where are those trees? There *is* something dark ahead. Why, I do believe the fog is clearing.'

It was. The light increased every moment and made him blink. The fog lifted. He was utterly in an unknown valley and the sea was nowhere in sight.   5

At that very moment the others were washing their hands and faces in the river and generally getting ready for dinner and a rest. The work had gone well so far and it was a merry meal. Only after the second helping of goat did Edmund say, 'Where's that blighter Eustace?'

Meanwhile Eustace stared round the unknown valley. It was so narrow and deep,   10
and the precipices which surrounded it so sheer, that it was like a huge pit or trench.

Eustace realised of course that in the fog he had come down the wrong side of
the ridge, so he turned at once to see about getting back. But as soon as he had
looked he shuddered. Apparently he had by amazing luck found the only possible
way down – a long green spit of land, horribly steep and narrow, with precipices on   15
either side. There was no other possible way of getting back. But could he do it,
now that he saw what it was really like? His head swam at the very thought of it. He
turned round again, thinking that at any rate he'd better have a good drink from the
pool first. But as soon as he had turned and before he had taken a step forward
into the valley he heard a noise behind him. It was only a small noise but it sounded   20
loud in that immense silence. It froze him dead still where he stood for a second.
Then he slewed round his head and looked.

At the bottom of the cliff a little on his left hand was a low, dark hole – the entrance
to a cave perhaps. And out of this two thin wisps of smoke were coming. And the
loose stones just beneath the dark hollow were moving (that was the noise he had   25
heard) just as if something were crawling in the dark behind them.

Something *was* crawling. Worse still, something was coming out. Edmund or Lucy
or you would have recognised it at once, but Eustace had read none of the right
books. The thing that came out of the cave was something he had never even
imagined – a long lead-coloured snout, dull red eyes, no feathers or fur, a long lithe   30
body that trailed on the ground, legs whose elbows went up higher than its back
like a spider's, cruel claws, bat's wings that made a rasping noise on the stones,
yards of tail. And the two lines of smoke were coming from its two nostrils. He never
said the word *Dragon* to himself. Nor would it have made things any better if he
had. But perhaps if he had known something about dragons he would have been   35
a little surprised at this dragon's behaviour. It did not sit up and clap its wings,
nor did it shoot out a stream of flame from its mouth. The smoke from its nostrils
was like the smoke of a fire that will not last much longer. Nor did it seem to have
noticed Eustace.

From *The Chronicles of Narnia: Voyage of the Dawn Treader* by C S Lewis

Underline the correct answers.

1 What is 'scree'?

(a hillside of loose stones, a level area, another word for 'fog')

2 Was Eustace missed by the group immediately?

(yes, no)

3 What was the noise Eustace had heard?

(a fire crackling, his beating heart, loose stones)

3

Answer these questions.

4 How do we know that Edmund was hungry?

_____

_____

5 What is the meaning of the word 'immense' on line 21?

_____

6 What does the line 'Where's that blighter Eustace?' (lines 8–9) suggest Edmund's relationship with Eustace is like?

_____

_____

7 Why did Eustace hesitate about returning back up the ridge?

_____

_____

8 Why did Eustace not recognise the strange 'thing' as a dragon?

_____

_____

9–10 Describe in your own words how Eustace felt on seeing the dragon and why. Use evidence from the passage to support your answer.

_____

_____

_____

_____

7

Write each of these words in their **plural** form.

11 scarf _____scarves_____   12 wolf _____wolves_____

13 belief _____   14 handcuff _____handcuffs_____

15 wife _____   16 penknife _____knives_____

17 remedy _____remedies_____   18 motif _____motifs_____

8

Add *anything* or *nothing* to each of these sentences.

19 Brian was bored, he couldn't find _____ to watch.

20 'There is _____ to eat,' moaned Tracey.

21 The bag had _____ in it.

22–23 The twins called 'There is _____ to do, we can't find _____ to play with.'

24 Orin said the mess was _____ to do with him.

25 'I'll read _____ to fill the time,' said Kate.

7

Write a **definition** for each of these words.

26 nightmare _____

27 remnant _____

28 dawdle _____

29 gust _____

30 valiant _____

31 theory _____

32 ghastly _____

7

Underline the correct word in brackets.

D 6

33 The Gallop family (was, were) having a day out.

34 Nasar (have, will) pack his bag.

35 Hannah and David (will, were) planning to have a sleepover.

36 Ben left in a hurry but (was, were) there just in time.

37 We (have, shall) climb the apple tree when we get home.

38 They (will, were) going on holiday.

39 The girls (are, was) leaning against the shop window.

40 After the water fight Hugh (was, were) soaking.

8

D 6

Write each of these **adverbs** in a sentence.

41 anxiously

_____

42 fully

_____

43 soon

_____

44 wearily

_____

45 somewhere

_____

5

Copy these sentences and add the missing punctuation and capital letters.

D 1
D 4
D 5

46–48 on a bright warm day we like to go to the park

_____

_____

49–52 when I play with Jack my pet dog I usually get tired before he does

_____

_____

_____

53–56 nina bought some pens pencils rubbers and a ruler before the first day of school

_____

_____

Complete each expression with an **antonym**.

57 ups and _____

58 through _____ and thin

59 _____ and white

60 coming and _____

61 take the _____ with the smooth

62 more or _____

63 _____ and far

Spell each of these words correctly.

64 exselent _____   **65** seperate _____

66 managable _____   **67** buisness _____

68 calander _____   **69** intrested _____

70 twelth _____   **71** quarelling _____

Underline the two **clauses** in each sentence.

72–73 I ran quickly up the street as Aunty Sam had arrived.

74–75 Helga put on her boots because she loved to splash in puddles.

76–77 Guy walked off in the opposite direction after he lost his tennis match to Hussan.

Next to each word write another word with the same spelling pattern.

78 strain _____   **79** rough _____

80 rouse _____   **81** stumble _____

82 ultimate _____   **83** tunnel _____

84 chord _____   **85** diverse _____

Write whether each word is a **noun** or a **verb**.

D 6

86 sing   _verb_

87 insulation   _____

88 specialise   _____

89 discussion   _____

90 suspension   _____

91 concuss   _____

92 comprehension _____

7

Complete the following **adjectives** of comparison.

D 6

e.g.	quiet	quieter	quietest
93–94	slow	_____	_____
95–96	little	_____	_____
97–98	far	_____	_____
99–100	large	_____	_____

8

Now go to the Progress Chart to record your score!   Total   100

Phaeton desperately wanted to drive his father's chariot. He begged Helios, the Greek sun god, to allow him as he wanted to impress his friends on Earth. Phaeton wanted them to believe he was the son of a god. Helios agreed but there was a warning …

'… whatever you do,' he said sternly, 'do not try to guide the horses. They know the path and, if you do not bother them, they will ride in an arc across the sky, until they reach the safety of the stables in the West.'

He had time to say no more. The great golden courtyard gates swung open. Light began to climb into the dark sky and the restless horses leaped into the waiting blackness. 5

Helios watched as the wheels and the hooves made splinters of light which surrounded the chariot like a ball of fire.

Phaeton held on tightly to the reins. The chariot thundered into the sky with a speed that made his cloak stream out behind him. The wind lifted his hair and his breath came in gasps. 10

Gradually, though, he relaxed and he began to enjoy the power and the swiftness of his flight. He looked over the side and thought of the people woken by rays from the sun chariot. He laughed aloud when he thought of the power he had to control people's lives. 15

'Soon I shall be over my village,' he thought happily, but when he looked over at the ground below him all he could see were patches of grey, brown and green. He was too far away even to see his village, let alone his house.

In despair he cried, 'No one will see that it is me driving the chariot.' He gave the reins an angry tug and steered the great horses away from their path in the 20 sky. Nearer to the Earth they swooped. The stallions gathered speed and hurtled downwards. Too late, Phaeton remembered his father's warning, and he tried desperately to stop the furious flight. The horses, sensing that they were no longer controlled, galloped faster and faster. Their flaming nostrils sent fire licking onto the earth and sparks flew from their hooves. Flames licked buildings, and crops 25 withered and died in the heat. Huge rivers were sucked into the air and only barren, scorched beds remained.

People were in panic. Dust from the parched ground filled their nostrils. Soil crumbled around them. Where were they to turn for help?

Only the father of the gods, Zeus, could help them. Gathering what little they had to offer as gifts, the villagers streamed to his temple and begged for help. Their pitiful cries soon reached the great god and he looked down with amazement at the devastation. He saw the sun chariot racing in great swirls across the sky, the driver hanging on grimly.   30

Taking a thunderbolt, Zeus hurled it with great force at the frightened boy. It hit Phaeton and its power sent him spinning out of the chariot. His body twisted in space until it landed, broken, on the Earth.   35

At a command from Zeus, the horses returned to their proper path. Streaming foam from their bodies made a shimmering haze around them and, as night came, the hidden chariot dissolved into the West and the darkness.   40

From *The Lonely Boy* by Barrie Wade, Ann Wade and Maggie Moore

Underline the correct answers.

1 (Phaeton, Helios, Zeus) is the name of the sun god.

2 Before Phaeton set off on the chariot, Helios warned him to (hold on tight, let the horses guide him, relax and enjoy the ride).

3 What happened to Phaeton when Zeus discovered what he had done? (he was hit by a thunderbolt, he was asked to stop the chariot, he and the chariot were burnt by flames)

Answer these questions.

4 Why was Phaeton keen to drive the chariot?

_____

5–6 Using evidence from the passage, describe Phaeton's character.

_____

_____

_____

_____

7 Copy one line from the passage that shows that the chariot is a **metaphor** for the sun.

_____

_____

_____

8 What does 'barren' mean (line 26)?

_____

9 Write another word for 'scorched'.

_____

10 Describe in your own words the moral of this Greek legend.

_____

_____

_____

_____

7

E 2

Choose the correct **prefix** to complete each word.

tele   circum   bi   auto

11 _____centenary   **12** _____stance

13 _____mobile   **14** _____lateral

15 _____matic   **16** _____scope

17 _____vent   **18** _____marketing

8

D 5

Rewrite these sentences, adding the missing apostrophes.

19 Bens football had a puncture.

_____

20 They were thirsty, but the cows water trough was empty.

_____

21 It suddenly rained and the three girls coats were soaked.

_____

22 Marks finger hurt after shutting it in a car door!

_____

23 Aunty Sues family waved as they turned the corner.

_____

24 Dan lost his ticket for footballs greatest match, the Cup Final.

_____

25 Five groups designs were displayed in the school hall.

_____

7

D 9

Circle the words that do not have an **antonym**.

26–31 wall   late   London   deep   top   yellow
        careful   diamond   male   month   egg   stay

6

D 12

Rewrite these direct speech sentences into **reported speech**.

32 'Don't forget that you have homework tonight,' called the teacher.

_____

_____

33 'Where's the nearest toilet?' asked the tourist.

_____

34 'Help, I'm caught in the barbed wire!' screamed the boy.

_____

35 'Stop that ball,' Greg shouted as it was heading for the goal.

_____

_____

36 'I really don't like Mondays,' mumbled Seeta to her best friend.

_____

_____

5

Use words from the passage to complete the table.

37–48 The chickens had been put away for the night. It had been easy tonight as they obediently marched to their broken pen, following Jordan as he sneakily tempted them with soggy mashed potato from the evening meal into their home.

noun	pronoun	preposition
chickens	they	into

D 6

12

Put a *tick* (✓) next to the words spelt correctly and a *cross* (✗) next to those spelt incorrectly.

E 2

49 feirce _____

50 diesel _____

51 pier _____

52 conciet _____

53 greivous _____

54 perceive _____

55 viel _____

56 foreign _____

8

Rewrite the following correctly.

D 4
D 5

57–71 sashas eyes stared in disbelief standing quietly in a stable was her very own pony i dont believe hes mine she whispered her mother smiled because she knew sasha deserved him

_____

_____

_____

_____

_____

_____

15

D 10

Write the common **abbreviation** for each of these.

72 old age pensioner _____

73 centimetre _____

74 Great Britain _____

75 headquarters   ————————————

76 Prime Minister   ————————————

77 water closet   ————————————

6

D 2

Add an **adjectival phrase** to complete each sentence.

78 Tom washed his hands in the _____
water.

79 Danni kicked her _____ bike.

80 The _____
weather put them off walking.

81 The _____ car broke down
once again.

82 Wusai ate the _____ cake hurriedly.

83 Jeremy awoke disturbed after having a _____
nightmare.

6

C 4

Write down three **onomatopoeic** words that can be associated with these.

84–86 thunder

————————————   ————————————   ————————————

87–89 train station

————————————   ————————————   ————————————

90–92 swimming pool

————————————   ————————————   ————————————

9

E 2

Add the **suffix** *ing* to each of these words.

93 hide   ————————————   **94** equip   ————————————

95 picnic   ————————————   **96** amuse   ————————————

97 test   ————————————   **98** enrol   ————————————

99 thief   ————————————   **100** separate   ————————————

8

After 37 years, polar explorer is brought in from the cold

On April 7 1909 the American explorer Robert Peary, nine months into an Arctic expedition, recorded an ecstatic entry in his diary. 'The Pole at last!!! The prize of three centuries, my dream and ambition for 23 years! *Mine* at last ...'

It was not, however, his. He was some distance from the geographic north pole and had not just become the first man to walk on top of the Earth. 5

Sixty years after Peary's disputed expedition, a young Briton named Wally Herbert led a four-man dogsled team to the pole, as part of an ambitious and still-unrepeated expedition to cross the Arctic Ocean on foot. In so doing, they became the rightful holders of the record that Peary had falsely claimed. 10

But while Sir Wally, as he became in 1999, may be one of the greatest explorers Britain has produced, he remains relatively unknown outside his field.

'To those that know, he is the man,' the polar explorer Pen Hadow said. 'He is the explorers' explorer, as Sir Ran Fiennes put it.'

In truth, getting to the pole was no more than an incidental ambition for the 15
explorer. On February 21 1968 his party set out from Point Barrow, Alaska, aiming to make the first ever surface crossing of the Arctic Ocean via the north pole. After 15 months on the ice pack – five of them in darkness – the men arrived in Spitzbergen in northern Norway, completing a journey of 3100 km (1926 miles).

'Ice core samples taken by a member of the party have become the benchmark 20
data for all studies into the impact of global warming on the polar ice caps,' Mr Hadow said. 'And that was just one expedition Sir Wally led. He also mapped something like 45,000 square miles, in three areas of the pole. He personally drew the maps, which are still the maps polar explorers use today.'

Taken from an article in *The Guardian* by Esther Addley

Underline the correct answers.

1 What nationality was Robert Peary?

(Norwegian, British, American)

2 In what year did Wally Herbert lead an expedition to the North Pole?

(1968, 1969, 1970)

3 When did Wally Herbert arrive in Norway?

(in daylight hours, in darkness, the passage doesn't specify)

Answer these questions.

4 Robert Peary wrote '*Mine* at last …'. What was he referring to?

_____

_____

5 Pick out the phrase from the passage which describes where the North Pole is.

_____

6 What is meant by 'unknown outside his field' on line 12?

_____

_____

7–10 How does the article make it clear that Sir Wally is an explorer worthy of note? Refer to the text in your answer.

_____

_____

_____

_____

7

Write two **compound words** that begin with these words.

D 11

11–12 mean   _____ _____

13–14 over   _____ _____

15–16 week   _____ _____

17–18 fire   _____ _____

8

Use each of these **prepositions** in a sentence of your own.

D 6

19 under

_____

20 in

_____

21 along

_____

22–24 List three more **prepositions**.

_____ _____ _____

Copy the passage, adding the missing capital letters.

25–34 having emptied the larder, uncle franklin returned to the rocking chair. he belched loudly, then grinned, trying to make a joke out of it.

mum walked in, in time to hear the burp. 'please frank, don't do that!' she exclaimed. 'isn't it time you were heading home?'

'i've missed the train,' he explained, 'thought i'd stay longer.'

_____

_____

_____

_____

_____

_____

_____

10

Write a **synonym** for each word in bold.

35 Meena found understanding the computer **jargon** a challenge. _____

36 We are having a **spell** of bad weather. _____

37 I was able to **persuade** my brother to lend me his mp3 player. _____

38 Moving house can be a major **upheaval**. _____

39 The swimmer **plunged** into the pool. _____

40 The head-teacher **seized** his mobile phone. _____

41 Jake **barged** into Henri. _____

42 The radio **broadcast** lasted for three hours. _____

8

Add a different **conjunction** to complete each sentence.

D 2

43 Sam and Tony hesitated at the door _____ they were afraid to enter.

44 Aimee wanted the large bag of sweets _____ she couldn't afford them.

45 Denali had to wait for the doctor _____ he was ready.

46 Jess knows it is recorder practice every Friday _____ she always forgets her recorder.

47 It was raining _____ Mum rushed out to collect the washing.

48 Alice went to Tuhil's house _____ Connor went to Fran's.

6

D 13

Rewrite these sentences without double negatives.

49 There weren't no parking spaces.

_____

50 I wasn't not going to the park.

_____

51 We haven't no money for the fair rides.

_____

52 There isn't no chance we'll make it for the start of the match.

_____

53 Jim hasn't bought no new coat.

_____

5

E 2

Write each of these words in their **singular** form.

54 safes   _____   55 scarves   _____

56 trousers   _____   57 heroes   _____

58 sheep   _____   59 crocuses   _____

60 berries   _____   61 shelves   _____

8

D 6

Add *was* or *were* in each gap to complete each sentence.

62–63 We _____ waiting for Tony who _____ not ready.

64–65 I _____ asked to play the lead role in the play and Sean _____ chosen to play my brother.

66–67 They _____ worried about the match with Forest School as last year

they _____ at the top of the league.

68–69 As you _____ late for the film at the cinema I assume it _____ impossible to get tickets?

Add the **suffix** to each of these words.

70 tasty + er _____

71 play + ful _____

72 easy + ly _____

73 employ + ed _____

74 spy + ing _____

75 buy + er _____

76 beauty + ful _____

77 merry + ment _____

Write whether each of these sentences is in the **past**, **present** or **future** tense.

78 I will be going to Disneyland in the summer. _____

79 We opened our presents quietly. _____

80 You're eating an apple. _____

81 He is leaving the house now. _____

82 The rain will soak the washing on the line. _____

83 This number challenge is very hard! _____

84 The clock stopped at 2.30 am. _____

85 The wind blew the tree down outside our house. _____

A number of words we use have been 'borrowed' from other languages. Complete the table below, putting the words under the correct country.

86–91 croissant   studio   schnitzel   ravioli   boutique   fahrenheit

France	Germany	Italy

Choose the correct **suffix** to turn each **noun** into a **verb**.

E 2

en   ise   ify

92 fright _____   **93** sign _____

94 solid _____   **95** fossil _____

96 glory _____   **97** apology _____

6

D 6

Underline the correct word in brackets.

98 He (has, shall) returned the library book on time so won't receive a fine.

99 Rachel (done, did) the dishes after lunch.

100 They (are, was) expected to begin the competition at noon.

3

Now go to the Progress Chart to record your score!   Total   100

Paper 12

By the shores of Gitche Gumee,
By the shining Big-Sea-Water,
Stood the wigwam of Nokomis,
Daughter of the Moon, Nokomis.
Dark behind it rose the forest,
Rose the black and gloomy pine-trees,
Rose the firs with cones upon them;
    There the wrinkled, old Nokomis
Nursed the little Hiawatha,
Rocked him in his linden cradle,
Bedded soft in moss and rushes,
Safely bound with reindeer sinews;
Stilled his fretful wail by saying,
'Hush! the Naked Bear will get thee!'
    Many things Nokomis taught him
Of the stars that shine in heaven;
Showed him Ishkoodah, the comet,
Warriors with their plumes and war-clubs,
Flaring far away to northward
    At the door on Summer evenings
Sat the little Hiawatha;
Heard the whispering of the pine-trees,
Heard the lapping of the water,
And he sang the song of children,
Sang the song Nokomis taught him:

An extract from *The Story of Hiawatha* by H W Longfellow

Underline the correct answers.

1 Where did Nokomis live?

(between a lake and a river, between a river and a forest, between a lake and a forest)

2 Is Nokomis, the daughter of the Moon, a young or old person?

(young, old, poem doesn't state)

Answer these questions.

3 What word in the poem means 'agitated'? _____

4–6 What was Hiawatha's cot made of?

_____

_____

_____

_____

7–8 What cultural group do you think this poem is about? Why?

_____

_____

9–10 Nokomis taught Hiawatha many things about the world in which he was growing up. Why do you think that was important?

_____

_____

_____

_____

Change these words into their **singular** form.

11 tomatoes _____	12 oxen _____
13 feet _____	14 mice _____
15 strategies _____	16 tables _____
17 penalties _____	18 gateaux _____

Write three sentences, each of which must include two **possessive pronouns**.
Underline each possessive pronoun.

D 6

19–20 _____

_____

21–22 _____

_____

23–24 _____

_____

6

Complete the table below.

D 6

25–40   jealousy   Bath Rugby Club   colony   dislike   gaggle   desk
       Iraq   flock   holiday   microscope   Keswick   beauty
       Charlie   puppy   love   bunch

Proper nouns	Abstract nouns	Common nouns	Collective nouns

16

Write an **onomatopoeic** word for each of the following.

C 4

41 a dripping tap   _____

42 a car passing at speed   _____

43 a spade digging in mud   _____

44 a fire burning   _____

45 thunder   _____

5

Write a **contraction** for each of these pairs of words.

D 5

46 they have _____

47 there will _____

48 would not _____

49 shall not _____

50 it is _____

51 I will _____

52 could have _____

53 does not _____

8

Write each of these pairs of short sentences as one sentence.

D 1

54 Monty the dog slept soundly. He was exhausted after his walk.

_____

55 Tariq received his swimming certificate. He swam 30 lengths of the pool.

_____

56 Sophie was very excited. She was having a sleepover at Helen's house.

_____

57 Dan dropped the books he was holding. Meena gave him a fright.

_____

4

Add the **prefix** *un*, *il* or *im* to each of these words.

E 2

58 _____patient

59 _____pleasant

60 _____literate

61 _____interested

62 _____legible

63 _____reliable

64 _____possible

65 _____logical

8

Rewrite the following correctly.

66–86 what are we going to do? i wailed we are really going to be in trouble this time

only if they catch us replied finn

but they are bound to i mumbled

_____

_____

_____

_____

_____

_____

_____

D 4

D 5

21

Write two words for each of the following word classes.

D 6

87–88 adjective _____ _____

89–90 pronoun _____ _____

91–92 preposition _____ _____

93–94 conjunction _____ _____

8

What is the **root word** in each word?

E 2

95 thoughtlessness _____   96 assistance _____

97 possession _____   98 assembly _____

99 unhelpful _____   100 computer _____

6

Now go to the Progress Chart to record your score!   Total   100

Progress Chart   English 9–10 years Book 2

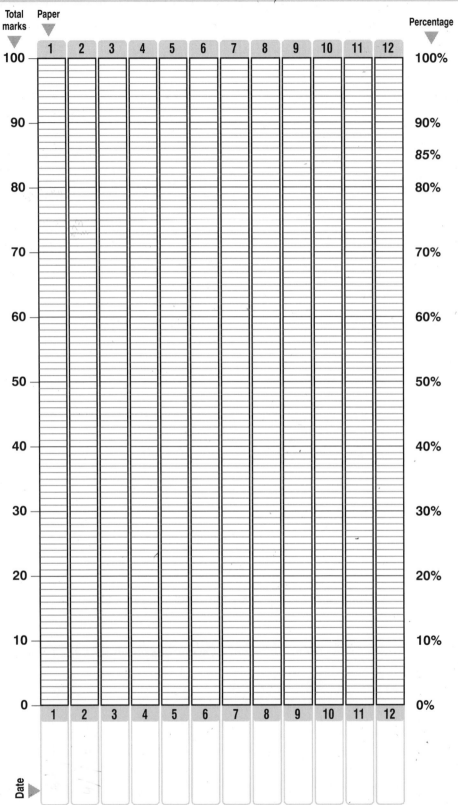

When you've finished the book use the Next Step Planner